Kiss the Earth When You Pray

APOCRYPHILE
PRESS

Also by Robert Hudson

The Christian Writer's Manual of Style, 4ᵗʰ Edition

Making a Poetry Chapbook

Companions for the Soul (with Shelley Townsend-Hudson)

Beyond Belief: What the Martyrs Said to God (with Duane W. H. Arnold)

Kiss the Earth When You Pray

The Father Zosima Poems

Forty-Two Meditations and a Prayer

Robert Hudson

illustrations by **Mark Sheeres**

The Apocryphile Press
1700 Shattuck Ave. #81
Berkeley, CA 94709
www.apocryphile.org

"On Prayer 2" was published in *The Other Side*. "On Prayer 4" was published in *Good Foot*. "On the Things of This World" and an early draft of "On Enlightenment" were published in *Christian Perspectives*. "On Intimations of the Afterlife" was published in *Opus 1*. Earlier drafts of "On Contemplation," "On Worship," "On Ancient Prayers," "On Silence," "On Praise," "On the Things of This World," "On Beauty," "On Dying," and the seven "On Prayer" poems were included in the privately issued chapbook *Listen! Twenty-One Nazms on Prayer* (Perkipery Press).

The front-cover image is an anonymous French painting dated 1880. Photograph by Shelley Townsend-Hudson.

Published in association with the literary agency of Credo Communications, LLC, Grand Rapids, MI 49525; www.credocom munications.net.

Printed in the United States of America

To Shelley,
Abbie,
Molly,
and Lili

and also
to Walt and Thanne

Contents

Learn these things.
When you are alone, pray.

Love to throw yourself down
on the earth and kiss it.

Kiss the earth and love it,
tirelessly, insatiably,

love all men, love all things.
Seek this rapture and ecstasy.

—Father Zosima
(Dostoevsky, *Brothers Karamazov)*

The Soul and Father Zosima

"What is the soul of a man?"

Blind Willie Johnson, the great East Texas guitar evangelist who recorded in the late 1920s, asks that question in one of his most compelling songs. It's a question that most of us ask from time to time and to which there is no shortage of answers. Theologians debate whether we *are* a soul or simply *have* a soul. Philosophers discuss whether the soul has an existence apart from the body or is co-existent with it—the old dualism conundrum—or whether it exists at all. Neuroscientists postulate that it's a neural illusion caused by a sort of feedback loop between the neocortex and the rest of the brain. Perhaps the soul is pre-existent, as William Wordsworth suggested in his "Ode on Intimations of Immortality," or maybe, ultimately, it is "conterminous with the universe," as Irish pantheist poet Edmond Holmes once wrote.

I don't pretend to know, though for me, Blind Willie Johnson, a true mystic among the old bluesmen, offers the most convincing answer: "It's nothin' but a burnin' light."

As a writer and editor, a lover of words, I'm fascinated by a different, though related, question: What language does the soul speak? If it speaks at all—and I have faith it does—it has to be in a tongue that has been spoken at all times and in all places, not only by the digital literati of our time but by the Paleolithic cave dwellers of Lascaux and the Olmec potters of Mesoamerica. That means that the soul does not speak the language of technology, science, politics, philosophy, or even ethics and religion. As important as those areas of life are, the soul, I think, lives elsewhere and speaks the local dialect of a country that is at once far more primitive and far more elevated than our own.

Here's what I'm getting at. The soul, I think, speaks the language of *awareness*—of which, I believe, there are four distinct dialects: the awareness of self, of nature, of others, and of the Other. Let any honest writer, painter, poet, sculptor, musician, or Blind Willie Johnson–style mystic begin seriously contemplating any of those things, and the soul can't stop talking. You can't shut it up. Those four awarenesses have been the recurrent chatter of our artists— and the universal themes of our existence—since humans first became conscious of being human.

That is the starting point for this collection. These poems, parables, prayers, and anecdotes explore what it means to be a mindful, created being in relation to self, nature, other people, and God. Although a confirmed Christian, I hope I have written about these things in a way that will appeal not only to my Christian friends but to my Muslim, Jewish, Sikh, Baha'i, and Buddhist friends as well. And even those who don't believe in a soul at all are warmly invited to listen in.

Other writers and artists have spoken that language far more articulately than I ever will, and I acknowledge the extent to which I've mimicked the psalmists, the gospel writers, the desert fathers, the Christian and Sufi mystics, the Zen hermit poets, the Beats, and many more. Overtones of all of them can be heard in the voice that speaks in these poems, though the unifying name I have given that voice is "Father Zosima."

Father, or Elder, Zosima is the beloved, venerable monk in Fyodor Dostoevsky's great philosophical novel *The Brothers Karamazov*, which was serialized in a Russian periodical in 1889 and 1890. The author died just a few months after its completion. The fictional Zosima, whose character was inspired by an actual Russian Orthodox ascetic of that name, was the spiritual mentor of the youngest Karamazov brother, the passionate, bright-eyed monk Alyosha. The entirety of book 6 is given over to the life and writings of the revered elder, and it is in those writings that he tells the young monks under his care to kiss the earth in prayer, to love all people and all creation, every leaf and every grain of sand. Father Zosima even dies, spread-eagle, face down on the ground, kissing the earth just as he'd preached. The spiritual struggle, the scandal even, that his death creates for Alyosha is one of the major, timeless themes of the book.

The short pieces in this collection are not meant to be a gloss on Dostoevsky's novel. (Who would even attempt such a thing?) Although I have appropriated the name and something of his voice, *that* Father Zosima is not necessarily *this* Father Zosima. While constantly addressing an unnamed *you* in imperative and sometimes imperious tones, these poems are how I talk to myself whenever I need encouragement, redirection, or a little healthy upbraiding, and I've found there's no better way to do this than to begin with an emphatic "Listen! ..."

Father Zosima's is a paternal, sometimes flinty, voice, quite different from that in which I usually write poems, and this is nowhere more evident than in the fact that Father Zosima seems to have achieved a level of spiritual maturity that I can only dream of. As C. S. Lewis somewhere said: It is one thing to write about the spiritual life; it is another thing altogether to attain it.

These pieces are my attempt to speak the soul's language, as inexpressible as that language may be. Ultimately, the language of awareness is beyond words, and in a few of the later poems in this collection (such as "On Praise" and "On Dying"), Father Zosima even tries to thrust words themselves aside so the soul can speak for itself, unhindered, in its own way. Such speaking, of course, is actually the path into deep silence, into contemplation, which is where this collection begins and ends.

My wish is that your soul too may yearn to speak that language of awareness long after you have forgotten the poems you are about to read. Or as Father Zosima himself says, "Love all men, love all things. Seek this rapture and ecstasy."

—Robert Hudson, Ada, Michigan, June 2016

Kiss the Earth
When You Pray

▓▓▓ On Contemplation

Let the soul wander
where it will, as in

an old pine forest—
no walls anywhere

but a thousand
thousand doors.

▌▌▌ On Enlightenment

There is light and there is half light
and both are holy. Listen—

one day a drunken man staggered
into a cave and fell asleep.

When he awoke it was night
and he could not find his way out.

He stumbled here and there
and wept because he knew

he would die in that darkness.
Then he fell asleep again.

In the morning he saw a dim light,
far off, filling the cave's mouth

but when he emerged,
the sky was overcast and stormy.

Though the sun was nowhere
to be seen, it was enough to rescue

the poor man from his plight.
So listen—here's what I'm saying:

you may never comprehend
the Holy One at all—

but you know enough to find
your way out of the cave.

On the Existence of God

A child came to me, looked
into my eyes, and said,

"Father, I'm scared …
what if there is no God?"

I thought for a time. Then
taking her small hands in mine

I said, "Listen—even then …
there would still be God."

On Prayer 1

People come to me and say,
"Father, how should I pray?"

and I say to them, listen—first
there is something you should know.

There was a man once
who had shells instead of ears

and night and day he heard
nothing but the waves of the sea.

And there was a woman once
who had stars for eyes

that could see forever in the dark—
but only in the dark.

And there was a child once
whose heart was a raging fire

and all it could do was burn
and leap upward with every beat.

Beyond that you don't need me
to tell you anything.

Just stand at the window
and lean your head out.

Let the mind be as strong
and invisible as wind.

And just pray. Just pray.
Then see what happens.

On Prayer 2

Some prayers are like spears.
They carry the whole weight

of the body behind them
but they do not travel far.

Some prayers are like arrows
flying light and far

and fast but they
are never seen again.

Some prayers are like snares
scattered in the woods,

ingenious and cunning—but
who knows what they will catch?

No. You cannot bring down
the Holy One with prayer.

He is not caught in your traps.
Listen—you are yourself the hunted.

Your prayer is the sudden stillness
on the path, the in-drawn breath,

the pounding heart
as you scent the wind.

Have you learned this?
Do you know?

You do not seek so much
as you are sought.

You cannot pursue the Holy One—
or if you do, it is only

as the fish in the net
pursues the fisherman.

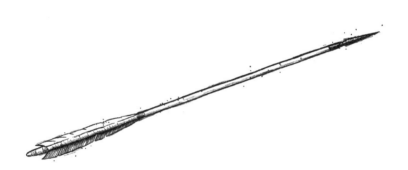

■■■ On Excuses

No—don't be like the man
who said, "If only I'd had

a fire to dry the flints,
I could have started a fire."

▇▇▇ On Worship

A man walked every day
to a certain mountain

where he would throw himself
on his face and worship

because he believed the mountain
was the little toe of God.

When the priests heard this
they came to see for themselves.

They laughed and said,
"You fool! Do you not know

that the Great Transcendent
Incorporeal Spirit has no little toe?"

And they scoffed and left him
to his weeping and devotion.

Later the man got up and went
to the temple where he saw

those same priests burning
incense and chanting prayers

and he said to them, "How is it
that the Holy One has a nose

to smell your incense and ears
to hear your prayers and yet

no little toe with which to tread
the earth? Tell me, is he lame?"

And the priests were so enraged
by his blasphemy

that they threw him from
the temple and stoned him.

So what am I saying?
Maybe just this: we all have ideas

about the Holy One—but they
are not the Holy One.

If the heart is unclouded
the temple is a good place

to worship, yes,
and so is the mountain.

▊▊▊ On Knowing Oneself

This morning a stranger
stopped me on the street

and called me by a name
I didn't know. "You're mistaken,"

I said but he insisted that we
had grown up together

in some distant village
I'd never heard of.

When I denied it again,
he still didn't believe.

"A brother, perhaps? A cousin
who looks like you?"

"No," I said and no sooner
had I convinced him

than he narrowed his eyes at me
and said, as if accusing,

"Lucky for you, for the man
I'm thinking of was a very great fool."

"Oh … ," I said and began
to wonder if he might be right.

▓▓▓ On Love

Where did you get this notion
that you are able to love?

That's like the eye saying,
"Sure, I can see. No problem."

But everyone knows the eye
is as blind as a dead mole for

it is only the one who peers through
its dark little void who sees.

Listen—the One who loves through
you is the One who loves.

On Gratitude

I saw a ragged old man
on the street today, who,

as he sprawled on his back
in the muddy wagon ruts,

looked up at me grinning
and said, "Well, at least

that's one less time
I'll have to fall!"

On Transcendence

Listen—these moments come
unexpectedly. In a blink, a twitch.

In the way the wind tastes
at the edge of sleep.

In a meteor half seen
in a corner of the eye,

more beautiful for being
rare and brief and doubted.

Or when you lean over
to pick something up

and from nowhere comes
the thought, "Heaven

is so easy." These moments
are as much as you

can bear, when the senses
let you slip and you become

like the forest deer who
leaps just high enough

to say, "There, I have left
all the world behind."

On Ancient Prayers

People come to me and say,
"But father, what about

the ancient prayers? Does
it do any good to repeat them?"

and I say, "You cannot make bread
without kneading the dough.

You must fold it and fold it
and fold it again.

But only when you
finally set it aside

can it be transformed
into something else."

▮▮▮ On Giving of Oneself

Listen—this is something you
should have learned by now:

the branch springs back a little higher
each time a cherry is plucked.

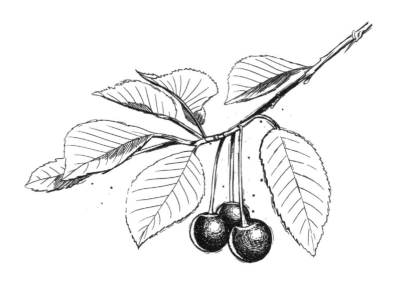

■■■ On Prayer 3

People come to me
and say, "Father, how

is it possible that prayer
changes anything?"

and I say to them, "Listen—
the whole world is shifted

from its orbit by a wren
lighting on a branch."

On Being Considerate of Others

Look how gaunt
the old fellow has grown,

as frail as twigs and
thinner than spring rain.

I ask him, "Why do you not
go out more, get some sun?"

"Because I don't want to scare
the children," he says.

▪▪▪ On Visions

As a child, I had a vision. No ... two.
In one, I held a thin piece of amber

to my eyes and all the world
was bathed in honey and gold.

In the other, I removed
the amber from my eyes

and every color blazed more
brightly than ever before.

Now, every day I ask—which
of these was the true vision?

░░░ On Pride

Once, a novice fell asleep
while eating a crust of bread

and an angel appeared
to him in a vision and sang.

When he told the others
the next day, they listened

in wonder and made him
tell it again and again.

But one old monk, Offime,
just snarled. "Nonsense," he said,

"you imagined it!" and he
stomped out of the refectory.

That night again the angel
came to the young monk

and again, when he told
the brothers, they were amazed.

Offime just slammed his cup
on the table and scowled, "Why

would an angel appear
to you? I've kept the laws

all my life and have never
been blessed with a vision!"

Again, that night, as the novice
was just about to drift off

to sleep, he heard a noise,
a scratching by his ear—

a sparrow was pecking
at his crust, chirping as it ate.

Next day he confessed to the others
(though Offime was not there)—

"I was only dreaming while a bird
sang in my cell," he said, then added,

"but as I prayed for forgiveness
I thought I heard the Holy One

whispering to me, far off,
'Listen—let's not tell Offime!' "

Looking up
through black water

what do fish make
of the full moon?

■■■ On Resentment

Years ago a celebrated poet came
to the abbey (he'd won prizes,

even medals from the czar)
and lectured us on how

to lead a spiritual life.
The brothers thanked him

and, bowing like willows,
smiled and clasped his hands.

I alone was resentful and
wrote a poem of my own:

"Oh, you stars may be luminous
in your worlds, but down here

even the fireflies outshine you!"
But soon I prayed to be forgiven

for my pride. Weeks later,
when I thought I'd forgotten,

the abbot stopped me in the hall
and pulled me aside. "Psst,"

he whispered, "what the hell
kind of poet wins medals?"

On Creation

There is this. The river, silent,
moving through the reeds,

the crab tree
crippled with fruit,

the doe in winter
that will die before nightfall,

and the sapling with ambition
in the heart of the forest—

all things are warm
from the forge of Creation.

The muskrat slapping
water with its tail,

the mute stones
wearing smooth in rain,

the earthworm lolling
from its hole in flood time,

and the night sky heavy
with snow but waiting—

all these are still warm
from the fires of Creation.

The ox at the yoke,
at the row's end, turning,

the yew and the heron
and the unwinding stars,

the swallow blinded
in the eye of the sun,

and the mole whose patience
undermines the world—

all these are still warm
from the touch of that Hand.

Who sows the seeds in the drops
of rain and fills the morning crows

with laughter? Who hung
the web in the spider's mind?

Tell every pilgrim you meet on the way,
the shrine of the Holy is everywhere.

■■■ On Silence

Shhh. Even
the pond frogs

know enough
to grow quiet

at the crack
of thunder.

■■■ On Prayer 5

Tell me, who taught you all
these long, patient prayers

full of borrowed phrases
and fine-sounding words?

You're like the man whose house
had one doorway—but no door.

To keep out the wind and the rain
and the cold, he piled old bricks

in the entranceway so that
every time he came and went,

he took them down
and piled them back.

One by one, in season and out,
he spent all his time

stacking and restacking. But that
can only go on for so long.

Sooner or later the One Who Listens
will scatter your bricks

with one fierce kick and grinning
like crazy say—"Anybody home?"

Invited or not, he'll upset
the plant stands, muddy the carpets,

overturn the tables, and sit
in your fat padded chair like a raja.

And when he moves in,
you'll be his guest—though prayer

on that day will no longer
be prayer. It will be Presence.

On Seeking Answers

How often we fail
to remember that

the simplest answer
may be at hand—

the water boiling in the pot
can put out the fire.

■■■ On Prayer 6

How many kinds
of prayer?

Three monks at harvest
stood in a field. One reaped.

One prayed. One gazed
at the south-flying geese.

▪▪▪ On Fear

Do not be afraid.
No path is unknown;

others have walked
there before you.

And even the pathless
path is not unknown—

for you yourself
are on it. Walk there.

On Vocation

The stone-deaf old gentleman
stands ready to light the fireworks

at the harvest festival,
just as he's done for fifty years.

Beaming like a full moon,
he slowly brings the touchwood

to the fuse and ... Whoosh!
KABOOM! *Crackle!*—

a sky filled with lights
and no sound, no sound.

On Listening to God

Do you think that
by leaning closer

to the sun, you are better
able to hear it burning?

Trust me. It's burning.
It's burning. Just listen.

On Rituals

I listened and listened
to the temple priests

quarreling about the proper
way to confer a blessing.

Some said hands must
be laid on the head

while others said two fingers
raised were sufficient.

When they turned to me
I said, "A feather's as good

as an axe if all you need
to do is chop air."

▮▮▮ On Prayer 7

An acorn falls from
the highest branch, tick,

tick-tick through
the dry unfallen leaves.

Quick, before it hits
the ground—pray something—

make it wordless,
thoughtless, a skyward cast,

the heart upturned into branches
of its own, if only to say

to the One Who Hears—look,
here I am, right now, just here.

On Mystery

Thinking only gets you
so far. The coyote is quick,

yes, but has she ever
seen a shooting star?

▌▌▌ On Time

"Too few hours in the day
to do what needs to be done,"

the novices were complaining.
"There's ministering to the sick

and tending to the poor.
There are children to be taught,

disputes to be settled, and work
to be done in the barns and fields,

to say nothing of prayer
and reading and meditation.

We hardly have time to sleep!"
So I decided to help them.

I removed all the hands from
all the clocks in the abbey

and said, "There, now you
have all the time in the world."

■■■ On Pilgrimage

Tell me—what are you
looking for if not

that place most distant
from yourself?

If you cannot leave
yourself at home

then you must lose
yourself along the way.

▮▮▮ On Seeing God

Look—if you can see
the whole of the moon

reflected, small as a pinprick,
in this bead of dew, then

surely you can catch a glimpse
of the Holy One peering back

at you from somewhere,
in some small corner of the eye.

▮▮▮ On the Things of This World

A mad old peddler
wanders from town to town

with a pack of priceless
trinkets on his back.

He can tell by just looking
in a person's eyes

what lusts and desires
lie crouched in the heart—

whether jewelry or carvings,
fine fabrics or books.

He can see at a glance
all he needs to know.

"Care to buy this ruby?" he says.
"See how it sparkles?"

"How much?" you ask
as he wades into your eyes.

"The price," he says, "is but
another ruby like itself,

of exactly the same size
and shape." He smiles.

"But there's no other ruby
like this," you say. "Are you mad?"

"Then here's what
we'll do," he says. "I will

make you a gift of this one
in advance of payment,

so then you will have a ruby
with which to pay. Yes?

Then I will leave this village
for a year—or a day—

and when I return you will
pay me in full. Agreed?"

So what am I saying? Just this:
the price of anything

in this world—is it not
the surrendering of itself at last?

And who even asks
the price of our desires

when the mad old peddler
is due back any day?

▮▮▮ On Perception

Right eye. Left eye.
That's all it takes

to make these stars
jump like crickets.

On Meditation

Smaller than the tip
of your finger, fish dart

in the rock-hollow runnels
underground. Be like that—

like a blind white cave fish,
smoother than eyes,

parting the water
with only its mind.

▮▮▮ On Beauty

A single thrush sings
in the open field

because she knows
all the world must die.

▓▓ On Praise

Tell me—these words,
what good are they?

You stick them up
like colored tiles

and take them down again.
But does all this talking

bring you any closer
to praising the Holy One?

If you give him your words,
why not give them indeed?

Use them once and let them die.
It is not prayer to slip the coins

from the merchant's pouch
to spend them over and over again.

Everyone knows that is thievery.
Be instead like the spoiled princess

who never wore the same dress twice,
who burned them night after night,

for only when she had
nothing left to wear but rags

could her lover come to her
at last and declare his love.

On Living in This World

This is the most
that you can do: walk

to a farthest point
and then walk back.

■■■ On Intimations of the Afterlife

You are participating in
something larger than your body.

The minute the doors began
to whisper escape, you suspected.

When your clothes jumped off
each night wishing to steal

your skin and smell, you
knew something was up.

When the body wished to open
on its spine like binding,

you said to yourself, "There is
more to me than I know." There is

more to you than a cough,
a bruise, a fear of windows,

a laugh so hot the lungs
have sidled shut. Now,

innocence is no excuse because
the signs were raw as hangnails,

persisted like jingles. Now,
when you lift your arms,

you move like a statue on wheels.
Listen—there is more to you than

the body ever let on, or the soul,
old scrapper, could admit.

On Growing Old

A time will come to sit
in the shadow of these trees,

shawls on our laps, too old
even to remember our names.

So let's try this. Let's write
"Holy, Holy, Holy, Holy"

on old scraps of paper and fold
them tightly into tiny pills.

For whatever Light awaits us
on the other side, surely

it can't hurt to have some
praises already on our tongues.

On Dying

There is this. No drawing
nearer to a voice but

always to that place
farthest from a voice.

Each word drawn under,
lost beneath the surface.

No speaking now but
water sliding over stones.

No faces now, no sun nor moon
to shine on flesh, but shadows

pacing here and there
and dim lights wandering by night.

The pilgrim merges with the way,
loses himself in leaves and moss,

counts instances of time
on the points of frost and dies.

His final ecstasy is this:
one dark tree falling slowly

through the arms of others.
But no, this is not death.

This is not dying. This
is the soul lying flat like a flood

and spreading itself evenly
over the world in a dream.

This is the fountain that was always
rising in the body, thin and red,

to embrace the million
forms into life at last.

A Prayer

Holy One, forever unfolding
like weather, forgive:

these grapes will not
ripen into wine.

They are too sour,
the flesh too thick.

So let me lay them in the sun
to sweeten for a time

and I will tell what I know
of seasons and sorrow,

of kindnesses untendered
and the soul's long wounds,

so that someday, perhaps,
when I awaken, we may

look into each other's eyes
and drink raisin wine together.

▮▮▮ Notes on the Poems

Epigraph: Fyodor Dostoevsky, *The Brothers Karamazov*, trans. Richard Pevear and Larissa Volokhonsky (San Francisco: North Point Press, 1990), 322. I broke the quotation into couplet stanzas.

Preface: Blind Willie Johnson (1887–1945); the song quoted is "The Soul of a Man," recorded in Atlanta, April 20, 1930. A copy of Johnson's gospel moan "Dark Was the Night, Cold Was the Ground," one of the most powerful pieces of music ever recorded, was famously sent into deep space aboard Voyager 2. From *The Complete Blind Willie Johnson* (Sony Legacy CD, 1993). *William Wordsworth* (1770–1850); the reference is to "Ode: Intimations of Immortality from Recollections of Early Childhood," *English Verse, Volume III: Dryden to Wordsworth*, ed. W. Peacock (London: Oxford University Press, 1972), 606–13. *Edmond Holmes* (1850–1936); the quote is from his book *Walt Whitman's Poetry: A Study and a Selection* (London: John Lane, Bodley Head, 1902), 64. Holmes is interpreting what he believes to be Whitman's view of the soul.

On Prayer 2: "... he is not caught in your traps ..." I have generally tried to avoid gender pronouns in relation to the deity, though for the sake of euphony, I opted for the traditional male pronouns in a handful of instances. I hope that the theme of God's all-inclusiveness is otherwise evident throughout.

On Prayer 3: The concept of the earth shifting from its orbit by a wren lighting on a branch was taken from one of Leonardo Da Vinci's marginal notes in his *Notebooks*. The second half of this piece is a found poem—and a haiku no less.

On Resentment: This poem is dedicated to friend and poet Brian Phipps, author of *Before the Burning Bush* (San Marcos, Calif.: Saint Katherine College Press, 2017).

On Vocation: This was inspired by a Chinese proverb: "Deaf Wang fires the cannon," from *Proverbs and Common Sayings from the Chinese* by Arthur H. Smith (Shanghai: American Presbyterian Mission Press, 1902), 139.

On Beauty: This poem is largely taken from a possibly misheard lyric in a Latin American folksong that I once heard on the radio. The precise reference is lost to me now, so if anyone knows what the song is, please contact me. Mishearing can be a wonderful source of odd and unexpected images.

On Intimations of the Afterlife: This is dedicated to professor and artist Gerald G. Boyce † (1925–1999) and was inspired by his exquisite silverpoint etching "When We Are No More, No. 10."

On Growing Old: Much of this poem came word-for-word in a dream and is dedicated to the memory of my late father, George "Ray" Hudson † (1919–2012).

▓▓▓ Acknowledgments

So many people to thank:

Shelley, as always, for everything. And Abbie, Molly, and Lili, of course.

Agent, scholar, and consummate bookman Tim Beals of Credo Communications.

Visionary writer, publisher, poet, pastor, and editor John Mabry of Apocryphile Books.

Brian Phipps, for his friendship and his bucking up, who said, "That voice *is* your voice."

Sarah Gombis, who came up with the title and was a much-needed encourager.

David Dalton, *il miglior fabbro*, for his indefatigable joy and energy. (I owe you more than you know.)

Leonard Sweet, for his love of contemporary poetry, which is an inspiration in itself.

Drema Hall Berkheimer, for her own beautiful writing and her encouragement.

Jack Leax, for his years of friendship and poetry.

Philip Yancey, who read an early draft of this manuscript and responded so positively.

Shari Vanden Berg, Mary Hassinger, Nancy Erickson, and Krista Fanning, extraordinary colleagues, for their kindness and soulful wisdom.

Artist Mark Sheeres for his beautiful illustrations. Subscribe to his online comic strip, *44th Street*, at http://www.44th streetcomic.com.

And Walter Wangerin Jr, for his many years of friendship and encouragement. I wouldn't be doing this if it weren't for Walt.

About the Author

Robert Hudson edits books for Zondervan, a division of HarperCollins. He is the author of *The Christian Writer's Manual of Style, 4th Edition*. He and his wife, Shelley, play fiddle and banjo in an old-time string band called Gooder'n Grits.